More Lies Ahead

TWENTY-THREE SELECTED POEMS

MARIA AMELIA MARCELLUS

Trafford PUBLISHING®   www.trafford.com
North America & international
toll-free: 1 888 232 4444 (USA & Canada)
fax: 812 355 4082

FIRST CONTENTS

SECOND CONTENTS

THIRD CONTENTS

LAST CONTENTS

I. In Nomine Patris

Am I too late
to stop myself
from needing hate
as now a new path
shalt navigate
shalt not deviate
follow me you said
more lies ahead

Do I pretend
to open my arms
letting nails descend
or offer my side
letting others offend
world without end
you for me instead
more lies ahead

And if I'm to show
what INRI means
above flesh below
will I apprehend
you as friend or know
that a cock must crow
to raise all the dead
more lies ahead

II. Roman Showdown
[Good Better Best]

Once,
for the good of all
one willingly came
giving;
a house, a world, a being,
a people, a mind, a past,
a mystery, and
the way.

Now,
for the better of another
some willingly leave
taking;
a home, a sphere, a soul,
a body, a thought, a future,
a story, and
the truth.

Soon,
for the best of one
all willingly return
needing;
a family, a circle, a spirit,
a person, a reason, a presence,
a message, and
the life.

III. Be Prepared

My brother and me
were allowed to play
on the sidewalk fronting
our brownstone walkupper
or in lampost shine cones
near the front stoop viewed
from fire escaper windows
away from hanging icicles
or on little square moze ache
tiles on the heavy ash trayed
landing level with finger
tracer marble bottoms going
halfway up to meet white
plastered and painted wall
rising the rest of way round
curving to the high arch top
perfect fit for a jump rope
real nice for Molly O'Dolly
or by the bold as brass
mailboxes with everybody's
buzzers and names but
none-as-neat as ours check
in the entry area vesta bulle
with lying mittens grabbing
as the old super would say
"no touchum plenty hot"
bang steaming radiator
sweating the snow off

until the wooly fingers stick
and might maybe even tear
or only on the car petted
hallway by Mrs. Koucic's
open door so then she could
be in and still keep a eye out
but never down there
where the stairs stopped
underneath coming to
a boxed no way out corner
where it was always dark
because someone took
the string off the light
and I wasn't tall enough
to reach the little chain

IV. Please, Oremus and Thank You

Our senses compete to remember
those big meals we all once enjoyed;
when everyone gave thanks for the plenty
and Dads were still there and employed.

Next we prayed, we hoped and we wondered
to Whom and for what should we care;
that soon these hard times could be over
for those choosing to earn their fair share.

But now you must carry each other
t'was a good thing we learned how to do;
and like us you'll need to start thinking
about teaching how all made it through.

V. Tailor Maid

Mean while world happens when she's alone
with innocent thoughts vesseled in a life told no
who will not matter before she wills an answer
like any worthy proposal knocking boldly enough
inside a royal carriage that either comes or goes
for she'll bring her skin to be next of grieving kin

Mean while world happens when she's confined
praying to a sky adorned in magnificent laboring
in well-rehearsed sunsets proud and made of steel
for another forever meal delivered in regal design
that kindness may create neither stripe or stranger
or another life told no laid in a neglected manger

VI. Et Filii [The Loneliest Tree]

Left to reason with sorrow
instinctively forbidden
to steer
anyone beyond
creation's reach
Only to satisfy experience
making, saving,
remembering,
a friendship known
but never shown

Left to ponder agony
with hope shaped,
tempered,
drenched in resolve
soaked in theory's sands
Only to carry another
balancing beaten heart
above and between
a grateful
and humbled mind

Left to open playful voices
that flutter about
the back porch
dancing, whispering,
turning the wrong key
Only to wait for footsteps
pretending to follow
tracks upon precepts
while emptying gladness
from the newest vessels

Left to watch wonder
dissolve in presence
diminish in joy
evolve in pain
escape in statute
Only to find oneself
warned of the darkness
that basks in sweet
Salvation
under the loneliest tree

VII. Any White Rose for Blue

So busy up to now
peddling to victory
or setting the table
never having taken
a long thought along
about any distant rising
roads and brutal hills
like any other cyclist
way backaway in the pack
who that plows for war
and plants for peace
heard 'bout them japs
hidin' sneakin' as they do
what happened where
when who sometimes why
they brought their grin
japs always bring
something to give or else
send their Love
from places yet to see yet
waste no words on what's
sure to be I suppose any
enemy can make their own
suppertime sacrifice
saving the best of the rest
of the rice for their own
holy day mourning

or surrendering the last
of their good white sugar
for what was meant to be
not just any Sunday morning
slant-eyed and buck-toothed
industrious and productive
nothing like shiftless jigs
or any other animal heirs
in the Kingdom yet still
he might have mentioned
something anything
any kind of Love is kind
ask any nip at the finish line
at least that's what I heard
but that's baby brother for you
he'll give 'em what for
and set their sun by god

VIII. Ubi Caritas

One then asks of two who are all gone,
why some others should take so long?
Modulating in voice, not meant to condone,
two now asks of one who was left not alone.
Was there no good found in our last request,
that left first for all, much better than the rest?
So ought not one want the best for all,
and hope that another will return your call?

IX. La Bonita Bendita [One Dollar Scholar]

Bendita
learn to ask for this
you do not want
Bendita
decide to seek for what
you already see
Bendita sea Dios
learn to touch
that which only others feel
los angeles
decide to be beautiful
for he who shall be cruel
cantan y alaban
learn to be patient
with he who can not wait
a Dios
decide to love
one who knows not how
commit to work
alongside they who will not
los angeles
and learn to be chaste
cantan y alaban
in a people laid waste

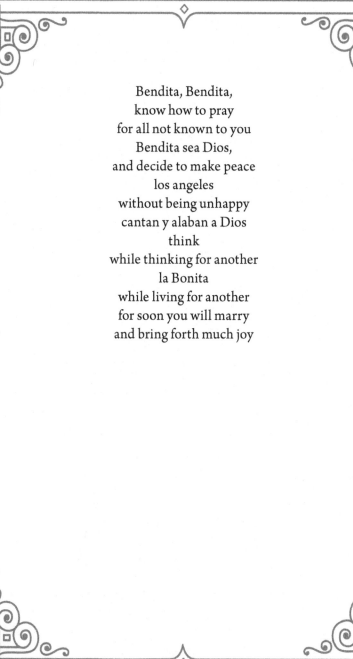

Bendita, Bendita,
know how to pray
for all not known to you
Bendita sea Dios,
and decide to make peace
los angeles
without being unhappy
cantan y alaban a Dios
think
while thinking for another
la Bonita
while living for another
for soon you will marry
and bring forth much joy

X. Notes Without Music

Why put a miracle away
when hope decides
it will no longer stay?

Why close another opened door
to end the dream
till it arrives no more?

Why take from me my hour
of desperate flight;
why keep me from my first
and final darkest night?
It's there
your love was meant to be,
and it's there
your love is truly meant for me.

So why store a promise
that you made
and not recall the debt
I haven't paid?

And why place a blessing
in my mind
then forget the tears
I'm now supposed to find?

So bring me to my first
and final darkest night;
then leave me to my hour
of desperate flight?
It's there
your love is all around,
and it's there
more miracles truly
will be found.

XI. Quo Vadis?

Bent along dim cobbled stair
gaze upon me pure dignity
fixed penetrating light
brightly borne and set fair
now clear and again after
wherever needed to bear

And when silvery darkness
too soon shall bring
a time to wrap quiet
safe for the Spring ---
Oh, carry what you will
to see perfection now drawn
then offer your last look
t'ward those leaving first dawn

Commit for me rather to miss
thy sweet farewell kiss
and taste love as sights blend
with these who now bend
for tonight eyes shall watch
while You dream the end

XII. Et Spiritus Sanctus
[The Holy Boast]

When he was
a young lad
attending
St. Agnes School,
they used to say
the commies
would wipe us out
if not prepared.

And he wondered
if anyone was
ready as he
with raw potato
and black licorice
stick wrapped in
waxed paper
stuck inside
his jacket pocket
over his jumper.

XIII. My Mortal Wiscon Sins
[Forward on New Avenue]

Who was the one who
said "Good-Bye"
as I was taken from
silenced and seated room
who was that had to be kid
unchallenged and courageous
outspoken intuitive dangerous
not applauded rejecting
split-decision-making
uncomfortable in the present
tense room amid many rooms
lifting nervous shaky voice
offering unlocked bars
with unmatched sincerity
absolute tribute that day
paid in full by one obvious
unknown soldier phrasing
fearless in youthful resolve
to form right questions
a will being done on earth
as it's supposed to be in Heaven
I shan't forget whomever it was
overcoming hesitation
validating kid perspective
ratifying spontaneous

developing "Good-Bye"
followed by my first name
when I was taken away
Who was the kid who risked
a cold war family reputation
in good Catholic standing
provoked by kid senses
experimenting with equivalence
exposed for the first time
to injustice
experiencing "Good-bye" from
heavy-handed high-ground
seizing abrupt early release from
the kid world world-view
who was that kid champion
by unanimous decision
that kid and me against the world
as it was in the beginning
who was it that knew more
than all others that day
Faculty notwithstanding
and made top grade
kid compelled "Good-bye"
a kid-reasoned decision
succinct in blessed context
to inject humanities morality
along with my first name
into abuse
and create authority
from the spoken word

XIV. Holy Angel in the Belfry
[Ad Majorem Dei Gloriam]

Like the town,
once steep'ld with vibrating
spires tolling strength;
our suspended sound
was fading---weakening
Veni Sancte Spiritus!

Ringing a memory
in pounded ear;
while striking an alarm
echoing, resounding
in loud pendulum time---
Veni Sancte Spiritus!

Hearing knotted rites
pass and stow beyond;
twisted high above,
pealing the dawn
from cracked hours
and blistered hands---
Veni Sancte Spiritus!

Hanging tones cast
stillness in silence;
listening for rythmic
melodies of Wisdom,
more deafening than
time's rolling chime...

XV. Forty-Four:
Extra-Ordinary Time

Made, gave, saved...
body, mind, soul!

Beg, borrow, steal...
here, there, everywhere!

Buy, sell, rent...
win, lose, draw!

Debt, pay, forgive...
red, white, black!

Trade, earn, own...
past, present, future!

Lost, seek, find...
Dad, Mom, Me!

Faith, Hope, Love...
them, us, all!

XVI. Sweet Land of Lost Sheep

She never saw much of her
Map and Pap.
They left home early
before she could wake
then returned late
as she lay sleeping.
But she knew they were damned-
good Americans
from the red, white and blue
marble cakes
that were remembered for her
that were taken for her
that were left for her
on the fireplace mantle
downstairs
in the living room.

XVII. A Means to Defend

Uniforms absorbing the
scent of Lent will eventually
don morrow a scene of green
kelly for you dee olive for me
moss rising up to meet thee
spies hope in ivy-covered envy

If only we were forest hunters
aspara Gus's or pistaci O'Tooles
sitting shady under the granny
toora loora smith scrumpy tree
two for tea and boy-o make three
in verdant repose beside I suppose

Algae fer thee and fern per thou
with sinners our Saint may allow
that I need be proud in this loud
emerald crowd afraid of resolution
so kiss me once and kiss me twice
'n kiss once a'gin fer Sinn n'fer Fein

Musha mish mush blarney said ye
to yer tired ol' rigid Mither McCree
pretending reliance in her defiance
awaiting monthly absolution
t'where I shan't blush out loud
with blessed light pea dissolution

tea hee how I twirl pine for you now
why because O'im an Irish good girl
And I don't dare give whisper
or outpour that I hate this war
because I'm a melting pot pearl
tucked inside a Catholic big sister
as my evening hair will unfurl
a new belief grown like an O'Leaf
so lettuce pay for all three ways
by faith begorrah and whisker

Will m'artie choke up spuds apeeling
minty fairies from limeys shading
the wind that's always got her back
worthy of mention in vanities like
sod and snake parting company to
unite odd people wee now folk recall
who used a torch to love our nation
by emptying bottles in sanities gob
so much mob for recrimination

Tiptop o' mornin' in ash offering can
let lyres in unopen pockets of sires
famish to banish and hide all the lying
till banshe belayin' in palm o' me hand
lest Father stand for another sham
for a rock that once plucked songs
is softly strung loose and lay dying

XVIII. Atom's Eve

Last night I saw my father cry
he was standing in the doorway
resting his right fist
halfway up
the paint-caked
wood jamb,
appearing so young
through the darkness
so I watched him
from the frozen aggregate
At the bottom of the stairs
all knowing this man
doubted he could be
a nation builder
or a war hero
as there are often
useful
less-sensational
more-reliable
better-suited choices
placed before him
choices that prefer
to play with life
choices that might
work best
spread out evenly
classically

like birthdays
but during this dream
he seemed like someone else's dad
not taller
not wealthier
not plainer than stiff
white aluminum siding
just somehow the wrong dad
somewhat different than the right dad
Last night my father knew how to cry
so I watched this dad
from the first icy step
knock on the front door
somehow not just another man
somewhat different from other men
and he was ashamed
looking at us looking at him
becoming relevant
through the cast iron railing
traditional yet ornately
popular when pounded
embellished with vines and leaves
that were patiently
chosen struck fired
inscribed storm-run
and rusted to perfection
decades before any New Dealers
would ever weld

XIX. Saecula Saeculorum, Amen
[Innocence Forever]

She played in the park with Jesus
He laughed as she grabbed for his hand
They had lots of fun on the swing-set
They scribbled pictures in the sand.

She walked for a while with Jesus
He cried when she wouldn't say please
They shared an ice-cream and soda
They slide safe and skinned their knees

She talked in the big woods with Jesus
He joked about working for free
They fed the birds all their breadcrumbs
They carved initials in only one tree

She splashed in the pond with Jesus
He watched the water drip from her hair
They argued about who threw the big rock
They got in trouble for taking a dare

She shopped at the boutique with Jesus
He spent it all on a clean white dress
They discarded the one that was ruined
They were sorry for the cost and distress

She danced at the party with Jesus
He sighed when she saw a new face
They both whirled and spun to old music
They then left Him to find a new space

She worked in the office with Jesus
He listened to all of her tears
They moved everywhere in right circles
They seemed to manage through the years

She escaped to the world with Jesus
He bled as He hung by her side
They fought every temptation together
They often found themselves opened wide

She ran through the wind with Jesus
He spoke without making a sound
They remembered it was only a pebble
They put the rock back on solid ground

She slept in the darkness with Jesus
He decided it was time that she heal
They explained they had a good reason
They needed others to know how to feel

She traveled a long way with Jesus
He smiled as she grabbed for his hand
They returned to their old playground
They found new pictures drawn in the sand

XX. High-Fidelity at Varsity Falls

After a year of
digging and chipping
and digging down
and shoveling away
and picking down
and chipping away
down and through
countless spaces
in solid Rock
we were shocked
astonished
and we were amazed
to find our
gold pocket watch
still ticking
still measuring
still tolerating
perfection

And right there
with clenched fists
hard posture
in the fullest moment
of Absolute time
we with grit teeth
angry breath
with sincere hearts

we again made
blame certain forever
and with the heels
of our worn out shoes
and with the soles
of our worn out boots
we again made
innocently certain
and this time
forever Amen

XXI. Bourgeois Cosmology

Thinking of someone,
when wisdom
becomes lost.
Remembering sometime,
how hope
will understand.
Living someday,
where commissioned
nature allows.
Knowing something,
why rooms
remain darkened.
Wondering someday,
who honors
greater glory.
Changing somewhat,
which crop
fears harvest.
Sensing somewhere,
when shame
becomes wisdom.
Believing somehow,
what's left
to faith.

XXII. Waiting For Last Chance Autumn

Paths too narrow
to sleep between trees
carry merciful forgiveness
and still-woodland dreams
Some find no room
for that loathsome thorn
or the tumbling leaves
that drop from once proud
and glorious autumns
Others squeeze their way
and might just have
room just enough
to collect then take away
all the sins of the world
narrowing further
yet still more-likely
to bear a false witness
or two from time-to-time
buffered by these stilled trails
standing under pressure
whip-slapping stinging branches
and leafy beaten bushes
speak of nothing but each other
painful on-going remembrance that
guide along ways too poor

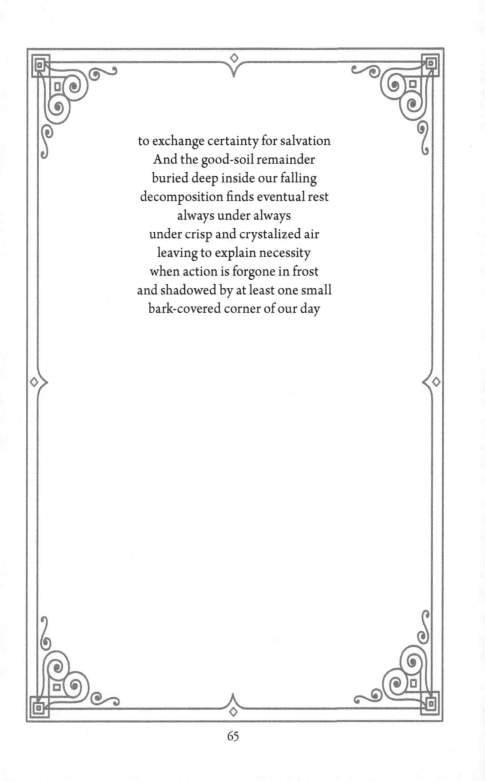

to exchange certainty for salvation
And the good-soil remainder
buried deep inside our falling
decomposition finds eventual rest
always under always
under crisp and crystalized air
leaving to explain necessity
when action is forgone in frost
and shadowed by at least one small
bark-covered corner of our day

XXIII. There Will Be Ghosts

One knee deep in troubled time
accustomed to asking for smaller portions
having learned to recognize apostles
wasting no dark gray sky on misery
having been taught to recognize pretense
and sort out apostles from apostates
and this is brought before you now
and this now you stretch out before me
now as though nothing now was ever before us
home fires and blue skies turned inside out
like these jealous snowflakes accumulating
nervously on our impatient skin congealing
to disturb the flesh stretched out before me now
as though nothing now was ever after us
but you will be seen dipped and tempered
in unselfish purity then fired with honor
for soon there will be nightmares
from places that can never remain hidden
so good night to peace but keep watch for me
and I will be seen kneeling and begging pardon
from only they that shamelessly sinned
as there will always be fears being always
on your footsteps and beyond your doorsteps
so good night to apology and find me
where there has always been ghosts
and we will remember what was said
in that one place we were taught contrition

in that same one place we were warned
aye, and there will be ghosts you'll be seeing
pretending in all the old familiar places
and yourselves shall never be lonesome again
in all the old familiar sing sing singing promises
in all the old familiar pretending places
standing together deep in some troubled time
after being taught how to be decent
after learning how to be loyal to each his own
pretending as though nothing now was ever
before us like the infinite sunshine accumulating
brilliant rainbows against our silver linings
but you will be known by allegiance to suffering
affection for duty your obedience to pain
and I shall be portioned out and remembered
as having eaten of bread I did not bake
and tasting wine I did not pour